D1368251

# MILITARY TECHNOLOGIES

# TECHNOLOGY DURING WORLD WAR II

HEATHER C. HUDAK

**Checkerboard Library**

An Imprint of Abdo Publishing
abdopublishing.com

# ABDOPUBLISHING.COM

Published by Abdo Publishing, a division of ABDO, PO Box 398166, Minneapolis, Minnesota 55439. Copyright © 2017 by Abdo Consulting Group, Inc. International copyrights reserved in all countries. No part of this book may be reproduced in any form without written permission from the publisher. Checkerboard Library™ is a trademark and logo of Abdo Publishing.

Printed in the United States of America, North Mankato, Minnesota
102016
012017

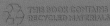
THIS BOOK CONTAINS
RECYCLED MATERIALS

Content Developer: Nancy Tuminelly
Design and Production: Mighty Media, Inc.
Series Editor: Rebecca Felix
Cover Photo: Library of Congress
Interior Photos: AP Images, pp. 8 (top), 17, 18, 29; Armémuseum (The Swedish Army Museum)/Wikimedia Commons, pp. 14–15; Getty Images, pp. 5, 25; National Archives and Records Administration, p. 21; Wikimedia Commons, pp. 6, 8 (bottom), 9, 11, 12, 22, 27


## Publisher's Cataloging-in-Publication Data

Names: Hudak, Heather C., author.
Title: Technology during World War II / by Heather C. Hudak.
Description: Minneapolis, MN : Abdo Publishing, 2017. | Series: Military
      technologies | Includes bibliographical references and index.
Identifiers: LCCN 2016944836 | ISBN 9781680784169 (lib. bdg.) |
      ISBN 9781680797695 (ebook)
Subjects: LCSH: United States--History--World War II, 1939-1945--Technology--
      Juvenile literature. | Technology--United States--History--20th century--
      Juvenile literature.
Classification: DDC 940.53--dc23
LC record available at http://lccn.loc.gov/2016944836

# CONTENTS

# ⟨1⟩
# THE WORLD AT WAR

**F**rom 1914 to 1918, much of the world was at war. Nations from around the globe fought one another in bloody battles across Europe. After nearly four years of fighting, the Treaty of Versailles put an end to the war.

Germany had been a major player in the war. But its leaders had been left out of the treaty discussions. And they felt its terms were too harsh.

The treaty required Germany to reduce its army, accept guilt for causing the war, and pay for war damages. It also had to give up one-eighth of its territory.

In the end, Germany signed the treaty. But many Germans disliked the treaty. Over time, German resentment toward the treaty increased. Soon, a new political party rose to power in Germany.

The National Socialist German Workers' Party, or Nazi party, was led by Adolf Hitler. Hitler blamed the Treaty of Versailles for most of Germany's economic problems.

Adolf Hitler gave powerful speeches that convinced people to follow his ideas.

He promised to end the treaty and help Germany return to its former glory.

In January 1933, German President Paul von Hindenberg appointed Hitler **chancellor** of Germany. Hitler gave himself the title *Führer*, which means "leader" in German. He declared himself the supreme ruler of the nation.

A fleet of Polish tanks and soldiers fight back against the 1939 German invasion that set off World War II.

In the mid-1930s, Germany broke the terms of the treaty. Other nations made little attempt to stop it. They didn't want to risk another war. This all changed in 1939. Hitler's Nazis invaded Czechoslovakia. Hitler planned to invade Poland next. The threat of war loomed.

On September 1, 1939, the Nazis invaded Poland.  Days later, the nations of Great Britain and France came to Poland's aid, declaring war on Germany.  Germany led the **Axis** powers.  Before long, other nations were siding with the **Allies** or Axis powers.  World War II had begun.

At first, the United States did not take part in the fighting.  On December 7, 1941, Japan attacked a US Navy base in Pearl Harbor, Hawaii.  The next day, the United States joined the fight, declaring war on Japan.

World War II lasted for six years.  During this time, bloody battles were fought across Europe and in Pacific Ocean countries.  During the war, both sides introduced new **technologies**.  From weapons to aircraft, both the Allies and the Axis found ways to improve equipment to gain advantage in battle.

Tanks were bigger and guns more powerful than during **World War I**.  A technology called radar made it possible to detect the enemy from far away.  And **atomic** bombs destroyed entire cities.  Some historians believe no other war in US history was more affected by advances in technology than World War II.

# TIMELINE

## SEPTEMBER 1, 1939

Germany invades Poland. Two days later, France and Great Britain declare war on Germany. World War II officially begins.

## JUNE 6, 1944

D-Day begins when **Allied** troops arrive on the beaches of Normandy, France.

## DECEMBER 7, 1941

Japan attacks the US Navy base at Pearl Harbor in Hawaii. The next day, the United States declares war on Japan.

**MAY 7, 1945**

Germany surrenders.

**SEPTEMBER 2, 1945**

Japan signs official
surrender papers.

**AUGUST 6, 1945**

The United States
bombs Hiroshima,
Japan.  Three days
later, it bombs
Nagasaki, Japan.

# 2

# ON THE GROUND

Ground battles were bloody scenes during World War II.  Armies from around the globe met face to face with guns.  Bullets flew across enemy lines as soldiers sped toward one another in huge tanks.

## TANKS

Tanks used in World War II were powerful war **vehicles**.  Their armored shells made them hard to destroy.  These massive machines ran on belted tracks.

These war vehicles had been used to storm battlefields in **World War I**.  Since then, both **Allied** and **Axis** nations spent a lot of money designing faster, tougher tanks.  Even before the United States entered World War II, it mass-produced Sherman M4 tanks for Allied nations.

The Sherman M4 tanks rarely broke down.  They had a main gun that could fire faster than most enemy tanks.

Sherman tanks were fitted with guns that could rotate 360 degrees.

And Sherman tanks were made with lightweight materials. This gave them more speed.

However, the lightweight materials also meant Sherman tanks were not well armored. Enemy fire easily broke through their outer layers. And the tanks often caught on fire. Fuel and **ammunition** stored inside a tank could explode from the heat of the flames. Crews only had seconds to get out.

While most of the **Allies** used Sherman tanks, Germany was known for its Panzer tanks. However, early models did not stand up well against Sherman tanks. In 1943, Germany put a new model, the Panther, into service. The Panther had thick armor that sloped on the top, back, and sides. Enemy fire couldn't damage it.

Germany also produced Tiger tanks. These tanks were slow, but they had powerful guns. They could take down the most heavily armored tanks. But Germany didn't have enough Panther and Tiger tanks to be effective. This was part of the **Allied** plan. The Allies had so many tanks that it was nearly impossible for the **Axis** to take them down.

## RIFLES

In addition to tanks, World War II soldiers used many types of guns for ground battle. One was the M1 Garand. It became the standard rifle for US troops.

M1s were strong, but built simply. They could be taken apart easily for cleaning and maintenance. They fired eight rounds, or bullets, before a soldier needed to reload. This allowed soldiers to fire more shots in less time.

These features made M1s one of the most important weapons of World War II. They gave US troops an advantage over Axis troops, which used Karabiner 98k rifles. Karabiner 98ks could shoot about the same distance as M1s. But they shot just five rounds before needing to be reloaded.

# M1 GARAND

The US Army first began considering the use of **semiautomatic** rifles in 1906. In the following years, several models were made and tested. In 1919, weapon designer John C. Garand began working on new ideas. The M1 Garand was tested over the course of many years. By 1937, it was mass-produced.

## LOADING

**1.** To load an M1, a soldier first pulled back on the operating rod with one hand. He then placed a **clip** of eight **cartridges** in the receiver.

**2.** The soldier removed his hand from the operating rod. This allowed it to move forward, and allowed the bolt to snap forward and close. This in turn caused the first cartridge to drop into place at the mouth of the barrel, ready to fire.

**3.** Next, the soldier pressed the safety into the trigger guard. The trigger is the lever pulled to expel the bullets. The M1 was ready to fire.

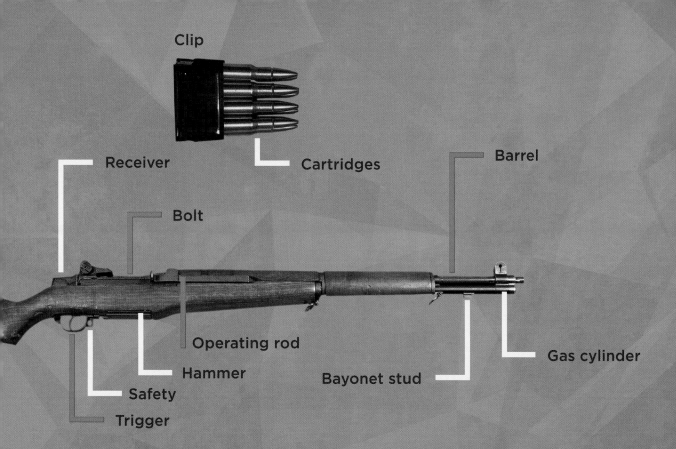

Clip

Cartridges

Barrel

Receiver

Bolt

Operating rod

Hammer

Bayonet stud

Gas cylinder

Safety

Trigger

## FIRING

**4.** To fire, the soldier pulled back on the trigger. The gas-powered M1 had a small hole in its barrel. When fired, some of the gas was sent toward a gas **cylinder**.

**5.** Near the cylinder was a piston attached to the rod, which was then attached to the bolt. The pressure of the gas pushed against the piston and bolt. This cocked the hammer. The bullet was fired, and the empty **cartridge** was **ejected**.

**6.** A spring then pushed the bolt forward. It stripped the next cartridge from the **clip**.

# 3

# IN THE AIR

**In order to win battles on land, troops often needed support from above.** The **Allies** and the **Axis** spent large amounts of money building aircraft. The United States alone built more than 300,000 planes during the war. And it used more than 100 types of aircraft.

Fighters, bombers, and transport planes were the most common types of aircraft. Most were made with lightweight **aluminum** and high-powered engines. This increased their speed, range, and altitude.

Fighters moved quickly and battled other airplanes. It was their job to drive back or shoot down enemy aircraft. Every few months, a new, improved fighter was introduced to the world.

The US-built P-51 Mustang is thought by many to be the best fighter plane of the war. It could reach speeds greater than 425 miles per hour (684 kmh) and carry ten **missiles**. It also had six guns, three built into each wing.

Bombers were heavier than fighters. They carried bombs long distances to drop on factories, military bases, and city centers. There were light, medium, and heavy bomber planes.

Light bombers were mainly used for bombing small targets with great **accuracy**. Medium bombers could carry fairly large

A Mustang had a clear bubble over the cabin so the pilot could see all the way around. External fuel tanks could be connected to the belly or wings. The barrel ends of the plane's machine guns were along the front edge of each wing.

The US army drops bombs from a fleet of B-17s over Dresden, Germany, in February 1945.

loads and were often used to bomb nonmoving targets, such as cities.

Heavy bombers carried large loads and were often heavily armored. To improve **accuracy**, most bombers used a bombsight. This device calculated a bomb's **trajectory** before it was dropped.

The B-17 bomber was a common heavy bomber used by the **Allies**. It was known as the Flying Fortress because it carried so many machine guns. The B-17 flew at high altitudes. It had heavy armor and a bombsight.

# THE BOMBING OF HIROSHIMA

Nearly all medium and heavy US bombers were equipped with the Norden bombsight. In testing, this bombsight was fairly accurate. More than 50 percent of the bombs dropped using this device landed within 75 feet (23 m) of their targets.

In reality, however, the Norden bombsight often missed its target. In many cases this was due to bad weather. Sometimes the plane needed to fly higher than expected to escape enemy fire. Other times, there was turbulence on the way to the target.

The Norden bombsight was used to drop the world's first atomic bomb. This bomb was more powerful than any other the world had seen. It was dropped by Major Thomas Ferebee from a B-29 bomber called *Enola Gay*.

Ferebee used the Norden to mark the target over Hiroshima, Japan. In practice rounds, Ferebee often missed his target due to miscalculations. On August 6, 1945, he dropped the 9,000-pound (4,080 kg) bomb. Its explosion destroyed 5 square miles (13 sq km) of the city.

## BOMBSIGHTS ON THE BATTLEFIELD

**Allied** and **Axis** troops also made use of noncombat aircraft. Transport planes were used to carry food, gasoline, and medical supplies to war zones. The people who built, flew, and maintained combat and noncombat aircraft played a key role in World War II victories.

# 4

# WAR AT SEA

**J**ust as aircraft **technology** provided advantages in the air, ship technology was vital to the success of sailors at sea. Landing ships transported people, **vehicles**, and supplies. Tankers carried cargo, mainly gas and oil.

Destroyers were common in World War II. These small, fast ships had light armor and small guns. They were often sent ahead of the battle to scout for enemy submarines and aircraft. Destroyers were also used to transport troops ashore and for rescue missions.

Battleships played an important role at the start of World War II. These massive ships had heavy armor and huge guns. Other advanced sea craft used during the war included cruisers and aircraft carriers.

Cruisers were larger than destroyers but much smaller than battleships. Like destroyers, cruisers could move quickly through the water. They had the heavy armor, fighting power, and the long range of battleships.

The USS *Pennsylvania* pushes through the Pacific as it leads another battleship and three cruisers toward the Philippines in January 1945.

Aircraft carriers were the largest ships of the war. They transported planes to the scenes of the action. Some carriers held more than 100 aircraft and had almost 3,000 crew members onboard.

The planes were stored below deck. Elevators brought them up to the flight deck. From there, the planes could refuel easily and then take off to join the fighting.

About half the troops who landed at Normandy were US soldiers.

Like aircraft carriers, submarines were important to the **Allies**' success at sea. They defeated more than one-third of the Japanese navy and 60 percent of its merchant ships. Several types of submarines were used during World War II.

# BATTLE OF NORMANDY

On June 6, 1944, more than 5,000 ships, 11,000 aircraft, and 150,000 soldiers landed on the beaches of Normandy, France. The attack was planned for months. The **Allied** soldiers stormed the **Axis**, taking them by surprise. This event became known as D-Day. It was the largest land, sea, and air operation in history.

Over the next several weeks, the Allies continued to push forward. They secured more and more land. Finally, by the end of August, they had freed France.

## SHIPS ON THE BATTLEFIELD

USS Gato-class submarines made their first appearance in 1941. They were nearly as long as a football field, and equipped with **torpedoes** and a deck gun. Beginning in 1942, Gato-class subs were also equipped with very effective radar.

On the water's surface, Gato-class submarines could move quickly. They had **diesel engines** that offered long range. But underwater, they were much slower. They used electric motors, and the batteries powering the engines lasted only a short time. The subs had to return to the surface often to recharge the batteries.

# COMMUNICATIONS

**W**orld War II **soldiers benefitted from advances in technology** both on and off the battlefield. Communications equipment was an important military technology. Staying connected was key to executing attacks. By the time the war broke out, soldiers and sailors used short-range radio devices to communicate from different battle locations.

Keeping information from enemies was just as important as sharing it with **allies**. The Germans used the Enigma machine to send secret messages to each other. This machine looked much like a typewriter. But messages typed into it were scrambled.

When a letter was pressed on the Enigma machine, a different letter was typed. Each day, the letter combination was reset. The person receiving the message needed to know the new settings in order to **decrypt** the message.

The Germans thought the codes would never be broken. But early in the war, **Allied** code breakers figured out how Enigma machines worked. Then, they could read the coded **Axis** messages. The United States had a machine similar to the Enigma.

It was known as ECM Mark II or SIGABA. By 1943, there were 10,000 of these machines in use. Enemies were not able to crack the machines' codes.

Enigma machines were easily carried, allowing Axis troops to use them on the battlefield and aboard naval ships.

# ATOMIC BOMBS

The **Allies'** invasion of Normandy, France, in June 1944 was a major victory for them. Over the next year, the Nazis began to lose power. On April 30, 1945, Hitler took his own life. On May 7, Germany surrendered.

The war was over in Europe, but it was still raging in the Pacific. Japan continued to fight. It became the target of the world's first **atomic** bombings.

During the war, many countries experimented with building different types of bombs. But no bomb was more powerful than the atomic bomb. In 1940, the United States began an atomic weapons research program. It was top secret, as many nations were also seeking ways to harness the power of nuclear fission.

Nuclear fission is a natural **phenomenon** that releases a massively high level of energy. Scientists wanted to harness this energy. They worked to turn this scientific principle into a powerful explosive device.

The United States dropped the first **atomic** bomb on Hiroshima, Japan, on August 6, 1945.  It killed an estimated 80,000 people. Three days later, the United States dropped another atomic bomb, this time on Nagasaki, Japan.  Another 40,000 people died.

The US bombing of Hiroshima and Nagasaki was the only time that atomic bombs have been used in combat. The United Nations would later call for the destruction of these types of weapons worldwide.

# ⫸⟨7⟩⫷

# SURRENDER

**T**he total destruction created by the **atomic** bombs helped lead to the end of the war. Japanese leaders signed surrender papers on September 2, 1945. World War II was over.

The cost of the war was high. Between 35 million and 60 million people were killed. Millions more were injured. More land was destroyed than in any other war in history. Even amid these losses, military **technology** helped pave the way for future discoveries.

Many of the technologies used in World War II became useful in future wars. Several weapons were employed in the **Korean War**, including Sherman tanks. Long-range bombers contributed to the design of planes that could carry hundreds of passengers. And discoveries about nuclear fission was later used in nuclear energy plants. No war has had a greater effect on our current technology than World War II.

Soldiers raise a US flag after a bloody 1945 battle in Japan. The attacks between Japan and the United States were the final battles of the war.

# GLOSSARY

**accurate** — free from error. The state or quality of being free from error is accuracy.

**allies** — people, groups, or nations united for some special purpose. The major Allies in World War II were Great Britain, France, the United States, and the Soviet Union.

**aluminum** — a silver-colored, lightweight metal. It is used in making machinery and other products.

**ammunition** — bullets, shells, cartridges, or other items used in firearms and artillery.

**atomic** — relating to atoms. An atomic bomb is an extremely powerful bomb that uses the energy of atoms.

**Axis** — countries that fought together during World War II. Germany, Italy, and Japan were the Axis.

**cartridge** — a tube containing the explosive charge and bullet or shot to be fired from a weapon.

**chancellor** — the chief minister of state in some European countries.

**clip** — a device that holds rifle cartridges.

**cylinder** — an object or space shaped like a tube.

**decrypt** — to change from a set of letters, numbers, or symbols that cannot be understood into words that can be understood.

**diesel engine** — a kind of engine that is powered with a special kind of fuel.

**eject** — to remove from inside something.

**Korean War** — a war fought in North and South Korea from 1950 to 1953. The US government sent troops to help South Korea.

**missile** — a weapon that is thrown or projected to hit a target.

**phenomenon** (fih-NAH-muh-nahn) — a fact or event that is rare or extraordinary.

**semiautomatic** — moving or acting partially by itself.

**technology** (tehk-NAH-luh-jee) — machinery and equipment developed for practical purposes using scientific principles and engineering.

**torpedo** — a submerged explosive.

**trajectory** — the path along which something moves through the air.

**vehicle** — something used to carry or transport. Cars, trucks, airplanes, and boats are vehicles.

**World War I** — from 1914 to 1918, fought in Europe. Great Britain, France, Russia, the United States, and their allies were on one side. Germany, Austria-Hungary, and their allies were on the other side.

## WEBSITES

To learn more about **Military Technologies**, visit **booklinks.abdopublishing.com**. These links are routinely monitored and updated to provide the most current information available.

# INDEX